The Way of God

Walking in the Way of Christ & the Apostles
Study Guide Series
Part 1, Book 1
A 6-Session Study

Peter Briggs

Daystar

Published by: Distributed in Africa by:
Daystar Institute / NM, Inc.   Daystar Institute / Africa
P.O. Box 50567   Kampala, Uganda
Albuquerque, NM 87181

www.DaystarInstituteNM.us
www.DaystarInstituteAfrica.org

Table of Contents

WitW

Walking in the Way of
Christ & the Apostles

Foreword

Jesus Christ, in His three-year ministry with His twelve disciples, modeled the method for teaching disciples to walk in His way.

The Walking in the Way (WitW) Study Guide Series attempts to model Christ's method of teaching by utilizing a holistic approach designed to challenge students to apply biblical principles to their lives and ministries. Our aim is to equip disciples of Jesus to "walk in him, rooted and built up in him and established in the faith, just as you were taught, abounding in thanksgiving." Colossians 2:6,7. Thus, we emphasize wholehearted discipleship, practical Christian theology, and a biblical world view.

We have prayerfully designed the WitW study materials to equip you with the tools and concepts needed to achieve this goal. May the word of God dwell in our hearts richly through faith by studying it, reflecting upon it, and allowing it to penetrate the deepest recesses of our souls. By this means, we bring our hearts and minds into alignment with God's heart and mind.

Using the Study Guide

Although this Bible study may be done independently, we strongly recommend using it in a group setting. Study each session prayerfully and reflect deeply on the included passages of Scripture as part of your daily devotional time with God. Establish a journal in which you record your answers to questions, as well as your reflections and notes.

If you are participating in a group study, be prepared to interact with your leader and group members. This includes sharing insights and practical lessons God is teaching you personally.

Read the questions and associated Scripture passages aloud and stick to the Bible as your sole authority for answers given. At the end of each discussion session, take time to pray for group member needs; then hold one another accountable for putting the lessons learned into practice.

Upon completion of one book, move on to the next book in the series. In parallel, begin sharing the WitW teaching with family members, work associates, and others in your circle of influence.

Leaders may use their discretion as to how much material to cover in any given discussion session. We also encourage Bible study teachers and leaders to read the associated WitW Theological Handbook or Theological Reader in order to gain a better understanding of the material presented in this booklet. Our resources are listed in the back of this study guide and are available on Amazon.com.

Introduction to Book 1 – The Way Less Traveled

The American poet Robert Frost in his poem The Road Not Taken writes:

"Two ways diverged in the wood, and I,
I took the one less traveled by,
and that has made all the difference".

The Bible in Matthew 7:13-14 encourages us to "enter through the narrow gate, for wide is the gate and broad is the path that leads to destruction." The narrow way, the one less traveled, is the way of Christ and the apostles.

Keynote Scripture

The keynote Scripture passage for the entire WitW study is this from the 2nd chapter of Colossians:

Colossians 2:6-7. Therefore, as you received Christ Jesus the Lord, so walk in him, rooted and built up in him and established in the faith, just as you were taught, abounding in thanksgiving. [Emphasis added]

Walking is an acquired skill. Toddlers are well-named, as they toddle around, unsure of themselves and their ability to remain upright. However, with practice, their confidence increases, their tumbling decreases, and soon they are walking and running.

Similarly, walking in the way of Christ is an acquired skill as we learn how to walk in the way of wisdom. Each small step of faith and obedience builds on the previous one.

Our desire is that every disciple of Jesus be firmly rooted, built up, and established in his faith. Our hope and prayer is that the WitW study materials will equip you with the tools and concepts needed to further your progress toward that end. May the word of God dwell in our hearts richly through faith by reading, thinking, and allowing it to penetrate into our very souls, bringing our hearts and minds into alignment with God's heart and mind. Indeed, our ultimate goal is that we would come to have and be governed by the mind of Christ in all of life and ministry (see 1 Corinthians 2:15).

As you begin each lesson, prayerfully ask God to open your heart to the study of His Word, to speak to you through His Word, and to allow the Holy Spirit through the word of God to break up the fallow ground in your heart. This study is not about learning a lot of facts – it is about the actual practice of the truth of the Scripture in order to glorify God and impact others for Christ.

Notes & Reflections

Formulate a statement of your personal goals and objectives for this study of the way of God. Also, make note of any additional insights or comments as you begin this study.

Session 1. The Way of Yahweh

Were you aware that from the very beginning there was to be only one way for all humankind – that is, the way of Yahweh. A second way was not part of God's original design. In fact, He designed man, not to operate autonomously, but rather to operate in continuous fellowship with his Maker. However, in stating this, we are in nowise suggesting that man's disobedience, as recorded in the 3rd chapter of Genesis, caught God off guard or took Him by surprise. But neither are we suggesting that God preordained man's disobedience.

In the 3rd chapter of Genesis, Satan penetrated the pristine environment of the Garden of Eden and introduced an alternative way to that of Yahweh. That second way was represented by the Tree of the Knowledge of Good and Evil. God had sternly commanded Adam not to eat of it upon penalty of death.

However, Satan deceived Eve into believing that the second way was to be preferred above the first. In fact, he characterized the second way as being at a higher, more godlike level of wisdom than the first. Sadly, Eve embraced Satan's lie. After she had eaten of the forbidden fruit, she convinced her husband to do likewise. Whereas Eve had been deceived, Adam's act of eating was in open prideful rebellion against God's express command. Only after he had partaken of the forbidden fruit did the impact of their sin come to bear.

Since then, humanity has been confronted with the reality of two ways, between which each of us must choose.

The Two Ways

I believe there is no clearer and more concise representation of the two ways than that expressed in the 1st Psalm.

> How happy is the man who does not follow the advice of the wicked or take the path of sinners or join a group of mockers!

Instead, his delight is in Yahweh's instruction,
and he meditates on it day and night.
 He is like a tree planted beside streams of water
that bears its fruit in season and whose leaf does not
wither.
Whatever he does prospers.
 The wicked are not like this;
instead, they are like chaff that the wind blows away.
Therefore the wicked will not survive the judgment,
and sinners will not be in the community of the righteous.
 For Yahweh watches over the way of the righteous,
but the way of the wicked leads to ruin.

Thus, we have...

The way of the righteous resulting in God's favor and
eternal life,

OR

The way of the wicked resulting in God's judgment and
eternal death.

This idea of two opposing ways permeates Scripture. There is but
one way which pleases God and which results in eternal fellowship
with Him; it is the way of the righteous. All other ways, as many as
there may appear to be, are contrary to Him, and they result in His
judgment and eternal death.

Before continuing with this study, we need to define two terms.
First, let's pay attention to the divine name used by the Psalmist in
the 1st Psalm. In most English Bibles, this name is rendered
"Lord." In the Hebrew Scriptures (i.e., Old Testament) the divine
name that is translated in this precise way is transliterated into
English as "Yahweh." This is God's personal or proper name. In
biblical passages that are dealing with God's intimate relationship
with His covenant people, this is the divine name that is most often
used. Such a passage is the 1st Psalm quoted above. Hereafter in
the WitW Study Guide Series, we will use God's personal name,
Yahweh, wherever appropriate.

6

Second, we need to define way as it is used in Scripture. This is a technical term in the sense that it is invested with a special meaning by the language of Scripture. It signifies a pattern of behavior or a lifestyle.

The way of Yahweh in the Hebrew Scriptures corresponds to the way of Christ and the apostles in the Christian Scriptures (i.e., New Testament).

Because of the connotation of the term "old" meaning worn out or discarded, we will be calling the Old Testament the Hebrew Scriptures, and the New Testament, the Christian Scriptures throughout the WitW study.

Carefully reread the 1st Psalm and then answer the following two questions.

Q1.   Describe the two ways or paths, including the companions to be found along each path and the results of choosing each path.

Q2.   How does one go about finding the way of the righteous?

Lest you are tempted to believe that the two ways are an artifact of the Hebrew Scriptures and are no longer relevant, consider the following passage from the 7th chapter of Matthew, which is part of the extended passage we call The Sermon on the Mount:

Matthew 7:13-14. Enter through the narrow gate. For the gate is wide and the road is broad that leads to destruction, and there are many who go through it. How narrow is the gate and difficult the road that leads to life, and few find it.

Q3.   Which of the two ways is more inviting and why? How is that way presented in your culture?

Q4.   Why would Jesus represent the Christian life as the narrow and difficult way?

Q5.   How does this passage counteract a common belief that if one accepts Christ, his life will be characterized by comfort, security, and prosperity?

The first mention of the way of Yahweh in the entire Bible occurs in the 18th chapter of Genesis, and it is associated with the patriarch Abraham.

Genesis 18:17-19. Then Yahweh said, "Should I hide what I am about to do from Abraham? Abraham is to become a great and powerful nation, and all the nations of the earth will be blessed through him. For I have chosen him so that he will command his children and his house after him to keep the way of Yahweh by doing what is right and just. This is how Yahweh will fulfill to Abraham what He promised him." [Emphasis added]

Q6.   According to this passage, what was Abraham to do in regard to keeping the way of Yahweh? How does this passage apply to us?

Another important passage that helps us better understand what is involved in our learning to walk in the way of Yahweh is found in the 1st chapter of Joshua. This passage records the manner in which Yahweh commissioned Joshua to assume leadership of the people of Israel after the death of Moses. The particular part of this passage upon which we will focus is the 8th verse, as follows:

Joshua 1:8. This book of instruction must not depart from your mouth; you are to recite it day and night so that you may carefully observe everything written in it. For then you will prosper and succeed in whatever you do. [Emphasis added]

In the Hebrew Bible, the word translated "recite" is *hagah*. In most English translations of this verse, hagah is translated "meditate." Whereas "meditate" usually denotes the action of silent reflection, hagah means something quite different; its range of meaning includes the action of audible, thoughtful recitation, which is how a person would go about memorizing Scripture.

Q7.   According to this passage, what are the keys to a way that is characterized by true prosperity and success?

Just as a child must learn to walk, so walking in the way of Yahweh – or the way of Christ and the apostles – requires instruction, training, and practice. Jesus Christ, the Master Disciple-Maker, spent three years with His disciples instructing, training, and

9

coaching them on the demands of being His disciples – that is, the demands of following Him and walking in His way.

Q8.   Do you think Christ requires any less of His disciples today? Explain your answer.

The last biblical passage we will study in this session is the 11th chapter of Hebrews. This is a record of the heroes of the Hebrew Scriptures whose lives illustrate the kind of faith that brings salvation. In fact, this kind of faith is defined by the biblical author in the opening verses of the chapter.

Read the 11th chapter of Hebrews in its entirety. Then consider the section on the life of Moses, which begins at the 23rd verse.

Q9.   How was Moses confronted with the two ways?

Q10.   Which way did he choose and on what basis?

Q11.   Based upon what you know about Moses' life, was his choice easy or difficult? Explain your answer.

10

Q12.   From what source did Moses derive the courage and patient endurance, not only to choose, but to persevere in the way of Yahweh?

Summary

In this session we have examined the historical background of the way of Yahweh and why it is important to walk in this way. We have seen that the idea of the two ways actually has its origin in the 3rd chapter of Genesis, and it continues throughout Scripture. The lives of the heroes of the Hebrew Scriptures summarized in the 11th chapter of Hebrews present important lessons for us in regard to not only choosing, but also persevering in the way of Yahweh, which corresponds to the way of Christ and the apostles in the Christian Scriptures. In this Study Guide, we will employ the term way of Yahweh when we want to emphasize that the way taught and exemplified by Jesus Christ was actually the ancient way in which Yahweh commanded Abraham, Isaac, and Jacob to walk.

Notes & Reflections

Record additional insights and comments resulting from your studies thus far.

12

Session 2. The Biblical Concept of Wisdom

In this session we will consider the biblical concept of wisdom and the relationship between the way of Yahweh and the way of wisdom.

Biblical scholars have noted the correspondence between the Book of Proverbs in the Hebrew Scriptures and the Epistle of James in the Christian Scriptures. Both present pithy and practical teaching on the way of wisdom. The Book of Proverbs does so within the framework of the Law of Moses, and James does so within the framework of the teachings of Jesus Christ as recorded in the four Gospels. Following is a key verse from each book:

Proverbs 9:10. The fear of Yahweh is the beginning of wisdom, and the knowledge of the Holy One is understanding.

James 3:17. But the wisdom from above is first pure, then peace-loving, gentle, compliant, full of mercy and good fruits, without favoritism and hypocrisy.

Q1.   Define wisdom as it is commonly understood in your culture. How does this definition compare with the way in which wisdom is represented in these two verses?

The following verse from the 111th Psalm imparts additional insights in regard to the biblical idea of wisdom.

Psalm 111:10. The fear of Yahweh is the beginning of wisdom; all those who practice it have a good understanding. His praise endures forever! [Adapted from the ESV]

13

Q2.   What does the Psalmist mean by practicing the fear of Yahweh? What is the stated result of doing so?

Read 1 Samuel 15.

This chapter records a pivotal episode in the life of Saul, the first king of Israel. In the beginning of the chapter, Samuel issues a command from Yahweh concerning the Amalekites. Because of the manner in which these people had been hostile toward the people of Israel as they journeyed from Egypt to Mt. Sinai, Saul was commanded to completely annihilate them, including men, women, children, and all their animals. Note carefully Samuel's rebuke of Saul in 1 Samuel 15:22-23 on account of his incomplete obedience to the command of Yahweh.

Q3.   If Saul had feared Yahweh in the sense of Psalm 111:10, what would he have done in response to Yahweh's command?

Q4.   In general, then, what is the essential manifestation of the practice of the fear of Yahweh in a person's life?

The biblical idea of the fear of Yahweh is a profound and worshipful reverence for Yahweh that invariably gives rise to strict, complete, and consistent obedience to His commands.

Q5.   What then is the relationship between the biblical idea of wisdom, the fear of Yahweh, and walking in the way of Yahweh?

The popular culture in the world views wisdom as being equivalent to cleverness or intelligence. In contrast, the biblical idea of wisdom is the practice of the fear of Yahweh that entails obedience to His commands. In other words, the biblical idea of wisdom is skillful living in accordance with the way of Yahweh.

Q6.   To what extent do we have an intuitive grasp of the way of Yahweh?

As we observed in the lives of the heroes of faith summarized in the 11th chapter of Hebrews, the way of Yahweh is both counter-intuitive and counter-cultural. In fact, it is radically so! Therefore, successfully walking in that way entails a lifelong project of absorbing and learning to consistently practice His word, even as Yahweh commanded Joshua in Joshua 1:8.

The way of Yahweh is the way of wisdom that leads to eternal life. Although it is counter-intuitive, counter-cultural, narrow, and difficult, whatever pain we experience in navigating this way is far outweighed by the glory that we will experience in the life to come. In contrast, the way of the world is broad, easy, and inviting. However, from God's perspective it is the way of folly, and it leads to ruination and eternal death.

In the first session we examined Joshua 1:8 as a cogent expression of the keys to walking in the way of Yahweh. Now let's fast-forward through Joshua's life and consider something he said near the end of his life, as recorded in the 24th chapter.

Joshua 24:15. But if it doesn't please you to worship Yahweh, choose for yourselves today the one you will worship: the gods your fathers worshiped beyond the Euphrates River or the gods of the Amorites in whose land you are living. As for me and my family, we will worship Yahweh.

The 24th chapter of Joshua records a covenant renewal assembly that Joshua convened to challenge the people of Israel to continue steadfastly in the way of Yahweh after his death.

Q7.　　Based upon Joshua's example, do you think the choice between wisdom and folly is a once-for-all choice, or is it repeated often as we make our way through life? Explain the rationale for your answer.

There is an interesting correspondence between this end-of-life declaration of Joshua and a declaration by the Apostle Paul that is found in the 3rd chapter of Philippians.

Philippians 3:12-14. Not that I have already reached the goal or am already fully mature, but I make every effort to take hold of it because I also have been taken hold of by Christ Jesus. Brothers, I do not consider myself to have taken hold of it. But one thing I do: Forgetting what is behind and reaching forward to what is ahead, I pursue as my goal the prize promised by God's heavenly call in Christ Jesus.

Q8.   What additional insights does the Apostle Paul impart concerning what is required in order to persevere in the way of Yahweh?

Summary

The Bible teaches that all of us begin our journey through life on the path of the wicked, the old way which leads to judgment, ruin, and eternal death. Each of us must make a conscious decision to leave that old way and begin to move along the new way, the path of the righteous which results in the blessing of God and leads to eternal life.

In this session we have examined the tight coupling that exists between the biblical ideas of wisdom, the practice of the fear of Yahweh, and walking in His way – that is, the way of consistent and complete obedience to His commands. We have seen through glimpses into the lives of Joshua and Paul that walking in the way of Yahweh is a lifelong enterprise. In fact, the genuineness of our faith is revealed, not by a one-time profession, but rather, by a life characterized by patient endurance to the very end.

Notes & Reflections

Record additional insights and comments resulting from your studies thus far.

Session 3. Practicing the Way of Yahweh – Part One

In the previous session we observed that practicing the way of Yahweh is a lifelong enterprise, requiring patient endurance to the very end. In this regard, consider the manner in which the author of Hebrews concludes his discourse on the heroes of the faith in the 11th chapter and opens his discourse in the 12th chapter.

Hebrews 11:39-12:2. All these were approved through their faith, but they did not receive what was promised, since God had provided something better for us, so that they would not be made perfect without us. 12:1 Therefore, since we also have such a large cloud of witnesses surrounding us, let us lay aside every weight and the sin that so easily ensnares us. Let us run with endurance the race that lies before us, keeping our eyes on Jesus, the source and perfecter of our faith, who for the joy that lay before Him endured the cross and despised the shame and has sat down at the right hand of God's throne.

Q1.   What imagery is imparted to your mind by the language of the Scripture passage?

Q2.   What is the implication of this imagery in regard to practicing the way of Yahweh, both individually and in community?

In the passage quoted above, the apostle seems to be depicting a cosmic relay race. Past generations of the faithful have run their laps, and they are now seated in the coliseum observing how we run our laps. However, their reward dangles on the thread of our faithfulness, since only together with us will they be made perfect or complete.

Some Definitions

Just as it is necessary for a medical doctor to study medicine and then put into practice what he has learned, even so it is just as necessary for the follower of Christ to study the Scriptures in order to learn about the way of God, and then practice walking in His way. The technical term for the study of God and His ways is theology.

The dictionary definition of theology is as follows: (1) the study of religious faith, practice, and experience; (2) the study of God and His relation to the world; and (3) a system of religious beliefs and ideas. The third definition applies to systematic theology, which tends to be sterile with respect to practice. The first definition best fits the WitW study in that it emphasizes practice and experience.

The word "theology" actually derives from two Greek words: Theos, which is the Greek word that means God; and logos, which is the Greek word that means word or discourse.

Therefore, theology is literally a word or discourse about God and His ways.

Practical theology is a study of God and His ways that seeks to derive from Scripture principles that should govern and direct our lives and ministries. This is what the WitW study is all about. Practical theology is something we do, not merely believe.

In fact, practical theology translates belief into behavior.

Doing Theology

I employ the term "doing theology" as the vernacular equivalent of practicing the way of Yahweh. It emphasizes the fact that our study of theology is very much an exercise of translating belief into practice. From this point onward, I will use "doing theology" and "practicing the way of Yahweh" interchangeably.

In this session and the one following, we will examine Scripture passages which guide and motivate our practicing the way of Yahweh both individually and in community.

In fact, persevering in the way of Yahweh is very much a communal enterprise as well as being a lifelong individual enterprise. Referring again to the Scripture passage from Hebrews quoted above, it is communal in the sense that our success depends upon our doing theology in community with Christian friends and associates who are running the race at the same time we are. And it is also communal, in the sense that our success depends upon our recognition that each of us is a vital part of Christ's universal church, with a unique purpose which God has ordained and prepared ahead of time that we should fulfill during our lifetime.

The biblical passages to be considered in this session are selected to guide and motivate our practicing the way of Yahweh both individually and in community.

Primary Source of Motivation and Instruction for Practicing the Way of Yahweh

In the previous session, we came to grips with the tight coupling that exists between wisdom, the fear of Yahweh, and obedience to His commands. The following three passages from the 10th chapter of 1 Corinthians and the 2nd and 3rd chapters of 2 Timothy impart motivation and guidance in this regard.

Read 1 Corinthians 10:1-13, a portion of which is quoted below. Then read the two passages from 2 Timothy quoted below.

1 Corinthians 10:1-6, 11. Now I want you to know, brothers, that our fathers were all under the cloud, all passed through the sea, and all were baptized into Moses in the cloud and in the sea. They all ate the same spiritual food, and all drank the same spiritual drink. For they drank from a spiritual rock that followed them, and that rock was Christ. But God was not pleased with most of them, for

21

they were struck down in the wilderness. Now these things became examples for us, so that we will not desire evil things as they did... Now these things happened to them as examples, and they were written as a warning to us, on whom the ends of the ages have come.

2 Timothy 2:15. Be diligent to present yourself approved to God, a worker who doesn't need to be ashamed, correctly teaching the word of truth

2 Timothy 3:16-17. All Scripture is God-breathed and is profitable for teaching, for rebuking, for correcting, for training in righteousness, so that the man of God may be complete, equipped for every good work. [Adapted from HCSB]

Q3.   In all three passages the Apostle Paul directs our attention toward what source for motivation and instruction in practicing the way of Yahweh as a lifelong enterprise?

Q4.   In 1 Corinthians 10:1-13 Paul cites episodes that occurred during what period of Israel's history?

Q5.   In 1 Corinthians 10:6 Paul states that these episodes experienced by Israel contain lessons for us. Then in the 11th verse he states further that they were written down for our instruction. Summarize the lesson that you derive from each of the episodes mentioned by Paul.

Q6.   What is the source of instruction for becoming an approved workman to which Paul points in 2 Timothy 2:15? What skill is needed to properly derive instruction from that source?

Q7.   What is the source of instruction to which Paul points in 2 Timothy 3:16-17? What are the benefits to be derived from receiving instruction from that source?

In all three passages, Paul states that the source of motivation and instruction for practicing the way of Yahweh successfully are the writings contained in the Hebrew Scriptures. In fact, the entire 11th chapter of Hebrews is devoted to summarizing the exploits of the heroes of faith whose lives are recorded in the Hebrew Scriptures. The most powerful source for motivation and instruction in practicing the way of Yahweh are the lives and experiences of those who have gone before us – especially those who have received commendation from God Himself.

In the first session you were directed to analyze the life of Moses, whom God commends as His faithful servant. However, as we will observe in Book 3 of this series, Moses faltered toward the end of his life, and he was thereby prevented from entering the promised land.

The life of King David presents many positive examples which deserve our emulation, but he faltered in the matter of Uriah the Hittite recorded in the 11th chapter of 2 Samuel.

Scan Daniel 1-6.

Daniel was a man who faithfully practiced the way of Yahweh from his youth until he was very old, and he did so under very adverse circumstances. In your perusal of the Book of Daniel, focus only upon chapters 1-6 which present a narrative of his life, together with the lives of his three associates, Hananiah, Mishael, and Azariah. (These three men are better known by their Babylonian names, Shadrach, Meshach, and Abednego.) In particular, focus especially on the manner in which these four men worked through adversity.

Q8. From your study of the Book of Daniel, identify three episodes that present especially powerful lessons for your own life and ministry. Identify the passage, episode, and lesson application. Record your insights by clearly stating the lessons learned, their application, and steps you intend to take for putting them into practice.

Passage / Episode / Lesson and its application

Summary of Our Study of Daniel. Daniel and his three friends manifest a fear of Yahweh which motivated consistent obedience to His commands in the face of circumstances which were designed to cause them to compromise. Moreover, they display a rock-solid conviction that Yahweh would deliver them from the wrath of the king, the intense heat of the furnace, and the jaws of the lions.

Scan the Sermon on the Mount, Matthew 5-7.

In the Sermon on the Mount, Jesus Christ sets forth the principles that should govern the life of a citizen of the kingdom of God. Thus, the Sermon on the Mount explicitly teaches us how to practice the way of Yahweh.

Q9.   Record the three most powerful lessons for your life and ministry presented in the Sermon on the Mount. As in the previous exercise, identify the passage, summarize Jesus' teaching, and briefly state the lesson and its application, including your intended implementation steps.

Passage / Summary of Jesus' teaching / Lesson and its application

Summary of Our Study of the Sermon on the Mount. The Sermon on the Mount includes the incredible promise that if we seek God's righteousness and the advancement of His kingdom as matters of first priority, then He will supply all our needs; therefore, we need not be anxious.

25

Of course, the ultimate example of appropriating this promise and practicing the way of Yahweh is seen in the life and ministry of Jesus Christ Himself.

Notes & Reflections

Record additional insights and comments resulting from your studies thus far.

Session 4. Practicing the Way of Yahweh – Part Two

In Session 2 we recognized the correspondence between the Book of Proverbs in the Hebrew Scriptures and the Epistle of James in the Christian Scriptures. James moves from one principle of practical Christian living to the next without any apparent ordering. In some passages he introduces a principle, and then he returns to it later, developing it further. We need to observe the amount of attention given to a particular principle throughout the Epistle in order to gauge its relative importance in James' mind.

Scan the Epistle of James.

Q1.   From your study of the Epistle of James, identify the three ways of most significance to your life and ministry in which James encourages believers to do theology by putting their faith into practice. Identify the passage, summarize James' teaching, and state the lesson and its application, including implementation steps.

Passage / Summary of James' teaching / Lesson and its application

From the beginning, God's design for the human personality has been that we would constantly lean upon Him for the wisdom needed to navigate our lives and ministries. This is what the Apostle James teaches in the 1st chapter of his epistle, beginning at the 5th verse. Notice how James' teaching parallels the teaching of Proverbs 3:5-6.

27

However, just as there are two ways, there are two competing sources of wisdom: that from below and that from above. James 3:13-18 sets forth the parameters of these two sources. The person who is practicing the way of Yahweh consistently manifests wisdom that is "first pure, then peace-loving, gentle, compliant, full of mercy and good fruits, without favoritism and hypocrisy."

A key passage on the relationship between works and the kind of faith that saves is found in the book of James.

James 2:14-17. What good is it, my brothers, if someone says he has faith but does not have works? Can his faith save him? If a brother or sister is without clothes and lacks daily food and one of you says to them, "Go in peace, keep warm, and eat well," but you don't give them what the body needs, what good is it? In the same way faith, if it doesn't have works, is dead by itself.

Q2. Based upon your study of the Epistle of James, and the passage quoted above in particular, how would you describe the relationship between saving faith and works?

According to James, the kind of faith that saves is invariably displayed through righteous behavior. A missionary leader shared the following statement some 40 years ago, which neatly summarizes the entire Epistle of James:

You only truly believe that which activates you.

This gets to the heart of our study. In the words of James, we must be doers of the word and not hearers only!

James 2:19. You believe that God is one; you do well. The demons also believe – and they shudder!

28

Q3.   How does this passage shed light on the relationship between saving faith and practicing the way of Yahweh.

What we really believe about God and His ways motivates how we practice the way of Yahweh. In fact, what we believe about God and His ways determines our values, our goals, our relationships, and how we use the resources God has afforded to us – especially the most precious resource of all, our time. The faith of demons is a theoretical faith – merely a mental assent – which has no bearing whatsoever on their behavior.

To summarize, the essentials of doing theology are:

Correctly understanding the meaning intended by the author in any given biblical book or passage.

Knowing how to accurately derive from the language of Scripture theological, moral, and ethical principles for governing and directing life and ministry.

Consistently applying these principles to our lives and ministries, and even our communities and cultures.

Being able to reproduce the results of our doing theology in the lives of other people within our circle of influence.

Doing theology in this manner should become a habitual and lifelong endeavor.

This figure illustrates four disciples doing theology in community over a meal. In fact, I am inclined to identify the man on the left as the Apostle John. Perhaps this picture was inspired by the language of Scripture in the following passage from the end of the 2nd chapter of Acts:

Acts 2:42. And they devoted themselves to the apostles' teaching, to the fellowship, to the breaking of bread, and to the prayers.

Another favorite passage of mine is found in the 3rd chapter of Malachi:

Malachi 3:16-17. At that time those who feared Yahweh spoke to one another. Yahweh took notice and listened. So a book of remembrance was written before Him for those who feared Yahweh and had high regard for His name. "They will be Mine," says Yahweh Sabaoth (i.e., the Lord of Hosts), "a special possession on the day I am preparing. I will have compassion on them as a man has compassion on his son who serves him." [Adapted from the HCSB]

Q4.   What do you believe these people were discussing that caused Yahweh to pay attention with pleasure, and even delight?

We believe they were speaking with one another about God and His ways. That is, they were doing theology in community. Following are two passages from the Christian Scriptures that further inform and illuminate the concept of doing theology in community:

Matthew 18:20. For where two or three are gathered together in My name, I am there among them.

Acts 2:46-47. Every day they devoted themselves to meeting together in the temple complex, and broke bread from house to house. They ate their food with a joyful and humble attitude, praising God and having favor with all the people. And every day the Lord added to them those who were being saved.

Q5.   What do these passages teach us regarding doing theology in community?

There is synergy in doing theology in community. As we share insights with one another, we all grow in our faith and encourage one another to greater faith, love, and action. This synergy is empowered by the Spirit of Christ, who imparts insights and

31

challenges that transcend what each group member individually contributes to the discussion.

Integrative Study Process

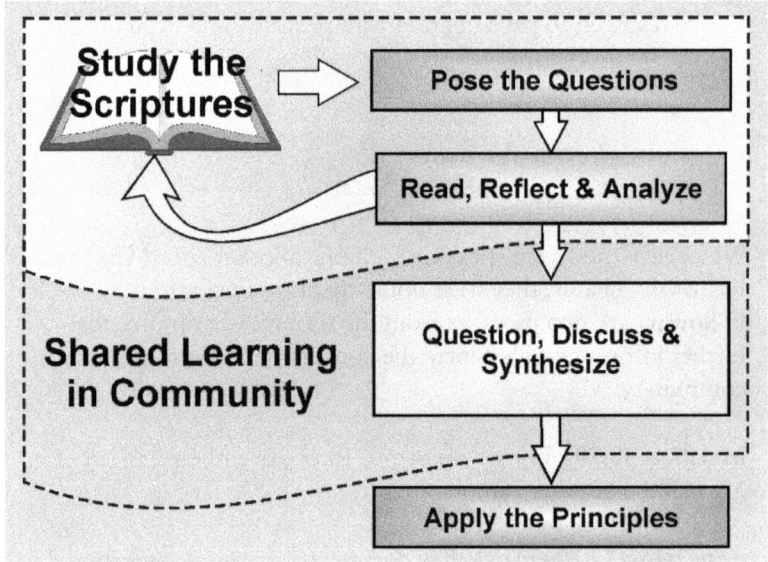

The way in which we practice doing theology in community is in accordance with the Integrative Study Process delineated in Figure 3. Doing theology in community is the learning environment Jesus chose among other options, and which He practiced in teaching His disciples. In fact, He practiced the ancient rabbinical model, which involves relational, life-on-life, in-service mentoring. The disciples observed His actions as He ministered, listened to His teaching, and questioned Him for clarification. Then there came a point that He thrust them out into ministry, to practice what they had learned from Him.

It is this same learning environment that we strive to practice in the WitW study through the use of the Integrative Study Process. We begin by studying the Scriptures, then move through each of the subsequent learning steps delineated in Figure 3.

Q6.   Reflect on the flow of ideas and concepts in this study guide and write a short paragraph identifying at least three ways in which the learning process you have experienced corresponds to that delineated in Figure 3.

Practical Suggestion

Find like-minded people in your family, at your work place, or in your neighborhood with whom you can discuss God and His ways. Then practice the Integrative Study Process with them by working through the WitW study.

Summary

The focus of this session has been on the practice of the way of Yahweh individually and in community. In Galatians 5:22-25 the Apostle Paul lists the ninefold fruit of the Holy Spirit, and in 2 Peter 1:3-11, the Apostle Peter lists the seven virtues of the Christian life that we should layer onto faith. Both lists present the profile of a person who is practicing the way of Yahweh, and, as a result, is living righteously. To simplify our discussion, let's condense these two lists down to just three virtues: wisdom, humility, and self-sacrificial love, where wisdom incorporates all the other listed virtues, including moral excellence, experiential knowledge, self-control, patient endurance, godliness, and brotherly kindness.

While we make a once-for-all choice when we respond to Christ's call into discipleship, practicing the way of Yahweh requires a whole succession of moment-by-moment choices whereby we learn to embrace and habitually practice wisdom, humility, and self-sacrificial love.

Notes & Reflections

Reflect on your experiences over the past week; think of specific points where you had the opportunity to choose wisdom, humility, and self-sacrificial love as opposed to folly, pride, and selfishness. How did you choose? What were the results of your choices?

Session 5. Say NO to CINO

A major motivator in creating the WitW study is to counteract
nominalism – that is, the state of being Christian in name only, or
CINO. We do not want to be CINO, but instead we want to be
authentic Christians who truly represent the character of Christ.

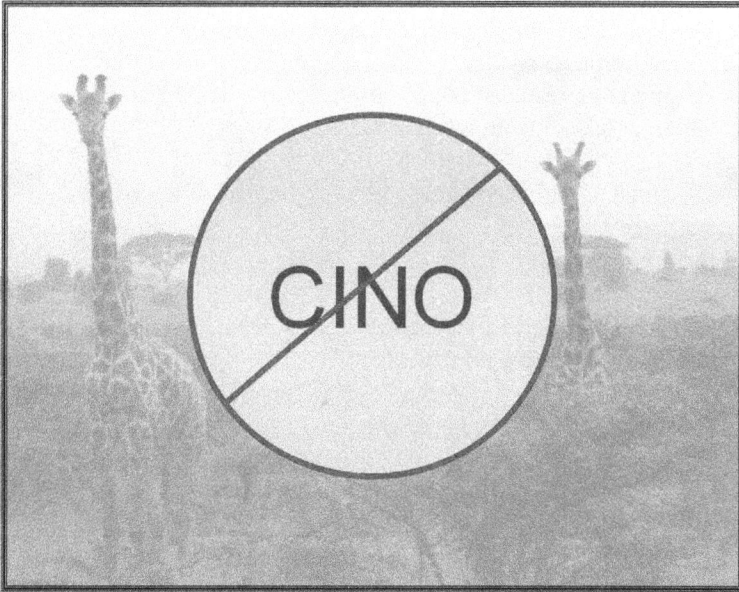

One of our African friends has observed that the theology
understood and practiced by the church in Africa is a mile wide,
but only an inch deep. We submit this is not only true of the
African church, but much of the church worldwide, especially in
the West. Deficient knowledge of the Bible and faulty application
of its teaching is the primary weakness of the church. Many
churches today preach a false or incomplete gospel. This results in
people believing that they are Christ followers but are not, people
who are not adequately equipped to walk in the way of Christ and
the apostles, and people whose lifestyles are not consistent with the
teachings of Christ.

There are at least two explanations for the CINO phenomenon. It may be that people are in this condition because they have never been truly born again and therefore have no personal relationship with Jesus Christ. Or it may be that they are immature believers who have never been established in the way of Christ and the apostles. This second condition can be caused by either or both of the following two factors:

A church community whose leaders are content to leave discipleship to chance, or who assume that discipleship will happen as a result of people attending the worship service and Sunday school from week to week.

Spiritual and intellectual laziness on the part of the believer.

Read 1 Corinthians 3.

Q1.   According to 1 Corinthians 3:1-4, what are some of the symptoms of spiritual immaturity?

Q2.   Describe the two kinds of people identified in 1 Corinthians 3:1.

The phrase "spiritual people" translates the Greek word **pneumatikos**, and "people of the flesh" translates the Greek word **sarkinos**. The life of the first kind of person is dominated by the things pertaining to the spirit, whereas the life of the second kind of person is dominated by the things pertaining to the body – in other words, material things. From what Paul states in this

36

passage, it is evident that when a Christian operates as a person of the flesh, it is a sign of spiritual immaturity. This is definitely an abnormal state, to which correction needs to be brought as quickly as possible.

Being a person of the flesh corresponds to the state of nominalism. One of the perversions of the Christian gospel that has arisen during the postmodern period (i.e., 1950 through the present) teaches that an obedient lifestyle for the Christian is entirely optional, and all that is needed for a person to receive the gift of eternal life is a one-time mental assent to the facts of the gospel.

A related teaching is that a Christian can operate as a person of the flesh for indefinite periods of time without impacting his eternal security. Both of these teachings are false! However, they have permeated the Christian community to such an extent that many of those people who attend the average evangelical church are CINOs – that is, people of the flesh.

Read 2 Timothy 3:1-9.

Q3.   What kind of people are being described in this passage? What, if any, is the relationship between these people and those being addressed by Paul in the 3rd chapter of 1 Corinthians?

We find the characterization of these people in the phrase, "holding to a form of godliness, but denying its power," most significant. In other words, those whom Paul is addressing in the passage are religious people. We take this passage as another Pauline characterization of CINOs – nominal Christians who are operating as people of the flesh.

37

Q4.   What effect do CINOs have on the proclamation of the Christian gospel, the advancement of the kingdom of God, and the way in which the Christian faith is perceived in the surrounding culture?

Q5.   According to your observation, what percentage of the people who attend your church are CINOs?

The CINO phenomenon contributes to the name of Christ, the Christian faith, and the Christian community being despised and maligned by the surrounding culture. A number of years ago, a prominent Christian leader was quoted as suggesting that as many as 75% of those who attend an average evangelical church are CINOs. Some CINOs deliberately infiltrate churches to teach falsehood and deceive believers who are not well grounded.

Colossians 2:6-10. Therefore, as you have received Christ Jesus the Lord, walk in Him, rooted and built up in Him and established in the faith, just as you were taught, overflowing with gratitude. Be careful that no one takes you captive through philosophy and empty deceit based on human tradition, based on the elemental forces of the world, and not based on Christ. For the entire fullness of God's nature dwells bodily in Christ, and you have been filled by Him, who is the head over every ruler and authority.

This passage includes our keynote passage for the entire WitW study, Colossians 2:6-7.

Q6.   What antidotes against nominalism are mentioned by Paul in this passage?

Acts 11:25-26. Then he went to Tarsus to search for Saul, and when he found him he brought him to Antioch. For a whole year they met with the church and taught large numbers. The disciples were first called Christians at Antioch.

Q7.   What did being a Christian mean to the first people called Christians?

Read Philippians 2:1-18.

Following Jesus is like being on a journey. From the moment we first heard and received the gospel message, we began the process of becoming more and more like Christ.

Q8.   List some essential attributes of a Christ-like personality according to the passage above.

Q9.   To what degree and how consistently are these properties exhibited in your life? Enlist the help of someone who knows you well in performing this self-assessment.

Indeed, as we follow Christ, we should become more like Him: in His humility, self-emptying, consecration, obedience, holiness, and self-sacrificing love. Let us examine ourselves so that we do not become deceived into thinking we are something we are not, or in thinking we are under His favor when, in reality, we are courting judgment.

Q10.   How does living according to our own natural desires and agenda compare and contrast with the model of Christ's life and ministry?

We need to close this session with three warnings:

Evangelism without intentional, ordered discipleship guarantees nominalism.

On account of the flesh, nominalism is the state toward which all of us tend, should we relax our spiritual disciplines. Thus, to avoid slipping into the state of nominalism requires constant diligence and effort.

Any given Christian community is, at most, two generations removed from slipping into a state of nominalism.

Let us ground ourselves in the word of God, and in James' words, "Be doers of the word and not hearers only." In this manner, we will become authentic Christians, and avoid being Christians in name only.

Say NO to CINO!

Notes & Reflections

Record additional insights and comments resulting from your studies thus far.

Session 6. Review & Discussion

Choosing the Way of Yahweh. In Deuteronomy, Moses exhorts the people to choose life. May we, as followers of Jesus, consistently choose to walk in the way of Yahweh, which is the way of wisdom that leads to eternal life.

Doing Theology. Although the terminology may be somewhat unfamiliar, the principle to keep in mind is that we must become lifelong students of the word of God, both individually and in community. We do this in order to develop in our understanding of God and His ways with the result that we are able to perceive the world through His eyes and respond to it in accordance with His mind and His heart. Learning about God and His ways takes a lifetime. Studying the Scripture with others under the guidance of the Spirit of God creates a synergy in which we encourage one another to walk in the way of God.

The Way of Christ and the Apostles Is Radically Counterintuitive. If we rely upon our natural intuition and lived experiences apart from God, we will fail. Only by habitually training our minds in the language, ideas, and principles of Scripture, and governing our lives according to its precepts, can we successfully live as disciples of Jesus Christ.

Just Say NO to CINO. The Christian who has allowed himself to slip into the state of nominalism and is operating as a person of the flesh is living, at least temporarily, as a functional atheist. In other words, he is living as if God doesn't exist. He is walking in the way of the flesh, gratifying its lusts; this is the way of folly, which ultimately leads to ruination and death. So long as he operates in this mode, he is advancing the kingdom of Satan, which is the kingdom of darkness.

We are not called to be Christians in name only, but Christians in reality and truth, practicing what we believe – that is, constantly offering to a watching world a personal translation of biblical truth into behavior that showcases the glorious grace of God. Such behavior offers a framework and a platform for our proclaiming the Christian gospel and expanding the kingdom of God.

43

Discussion Questions

Q1.   In your own words, summarize the purpose of the WitW study.

Q2.   Define the meaning of the biblical phrase, the way. In this study guide, we have examined the relationship between the ancient way of Yahweh, introduced in Genesis 18:19 in connection with Abraham, and the way of Christ and the apostles. In your own words, summarize this relationship.

Q3.   In Philippians 1:27, the Apostle Paul exhorts us to live in a manner worthy of the gospel of Christ. What is the relationship between this exhortation and our living in accordance with the way of Christ and the apostles?

Q4.   What is the significance of the fact that there are two contrasting ways presented in Scripture: the way of wisdom that leads to life, and the way of folly that leads to ruination and death. In Matthew 7:13-14, Jesus represents the first way as narrow and difficult and the second as broad, easy, and inviting. Based upon all your studies thus far, discuss the significance of this representation by Jesus.

Q5.   We can define theology as the study of God and His ways. Discuss what is meant by the terms doing theology and doing theology in community and why the consistent practice of these disciplines is vital to our success.

Q6.   Discuss the importance of instruction in our learning to practice the way of Yahweh. Does every disciple of Christ need such instruction, or only those in leadership roles?

Q7. List the concepts and insights that have been brought to your mind by this study guide. Of these concepts and insights, which three are the most important to you and why? How are you planning to reorder your life in accordance with these concepts and insights?

Notes & Reflections

Congratulations! You have just completed your first booklet in the WitW Study Guide Series. We trust you have found it useful and encouraging in your walk with Christ, and that you will be motivated to continue your journey with Book 2, The Storyline of the Bible.

Record additional insights and comments resulting from your studies thus far.

Afterword

WitW is a product of Daystar Institute of Biblical Theology and Leadership Development (DI), which is dedicated to supporting local churches in fulfillment of their mission of making disciples of all nations. We have two offices: DI / NM is based in Albuquerque, New Mexico, and DI / A is based in Kampala, Uganda. Please do not hesitate to contact us at www.DaystarInstitute/NM.us if you have any questions or comments or wish to request training in the use of our materials.

Peter Briggs is founder and president-emeritus of Daystar Institute of Biblical Theology & Leadership Development. In addition to teaching and mentoring, Dr. Briggs has authored the WitW Study Guide Series to challenge students in uncompromising discipleship, practical Christian theology, and building a biblical worldview. The WitW study has had a great impact in both East Africa and the USA and is an excellent tool for encouraging and equipping disciples of Jesus to actually live out their faith.

Dedication

The *Walking in the Way of Christ & the Apostles Study Guide Series* is dedicated to Reverend Morris Wanje, whose prayers for God to raise up a means for strengthening and equipping young pastors and church leaders in East Africa caused the Holy Spirit of God to move upon the hearts of godly men and women at Daystar Institute/NM to create this study.

Acknowledgments

I am grateful for the heroic efforts of our team of contributors, editors, board of directors, and all who have had a part in the development of the WitW study. In particular, I extend my heartfelt gratitude to my wife, Rosemarie, our daughter, Ruthanne Hamrick, and ministry associates John & Marcie Kinzer, Stephen Patterson, and Michael & Antoninah Mutinda, for their valuable input and help with the Study Guide Series; and to Darienne Dumas and Emily Fuller for proof-reading the texts.

Testimonials

"The *Walking in the Way of Christ & the Apostles* (WitW) series by Dr. Peter Briggs is a powerful tool for fulfilling Jesus' universal mandate to make disciples. WitW is theologically sound, conceptually brilliant, and life- changing for those who are trained by it. The impact of WitW is not only personal transformation into the image of Christ, but also a profound influence on families, churches, and the larger culture, whether in America or Africa or anywhere else. Peter Briggs is a theologian of substantial import, but he has not merely plied his theological craft in the halls of academia. With God's enablement, he has managed to translate biblical truth and disciple-making principles into something that actually works in the real world! Those who embrace and employ *Walking in the Way* in their own lives will find themselves part of a movement affecting generations to come."

Steven Collins, PhD, Executive Dean, Trinity Southwest University

"*Walking in the Way of Christ & the Apostles* (WitW) is a magnificent literary work in biblical theology that offers the student an education in practical Christianity. The WitW study was first introduced in November 2011; since that time we have been using it to instruct ministry leaders and rural pastors at a low cost, and the transformation of lives is phenomenal. Learners get to understand the message of the Bible and are able to study it effectively. In my own interaction with the material since 2012, I have come to realize that Jesus Christ is using it to revive His remnant in Kenya and other parts of Africa, teaching us how to think in a biblical way and be successful in all spheres of life. I am convinced that the WitW material holds the key to Africa's revival, and, in Yahweh's hand, it is a mighty tool for returning the continent back to Him."

Michael Mutinda, Team Leader, Daystar Institute / Africa

Walking in the Way of Christ & the Apostles
Study Guide Series

Part 1: Foundational Principles. These principles are foundational to equip the Christ-follower to have and to be governed by the mind of Christ.

   1. The Way of God
   2. The Storyline of the Bible
   3. Biblical Reality
   4. Discovering the Meaning of Scripture
   5. Torah: The Fountainhead of Wisdom
   6. The Two-Part Christian Gospel

Part 2: The Gospel of the Kingdom of God. Here we explore the ways in which the Christian gospel confronts the prideful rebellion of the human heart and exalts Christ as King over all.

   7. Authority of the King
   8. Called by the King
   9. The Meaning of Discipleship
   10. Disciplines of the Kingdom
   11. Household of the King
   12. The Second Coming of the King

Part 3 – The Gospel of God. This final set explores how the Christian gospel affords a complete solution to human depravity and the threefold problem of sin and death.

   13. Introduction to the Gospel of God
   14. The Reason for the Gospel of God
   15. Content of the Gospel of God
   16. Perversions of the Gospel of God
   17. Application of the Gospel of God

Theological Readers (TR)

   TR1 – Part 1: Foundational Principles
   TR2 – Part 2: The Gospel of the Kingdom of God
   TR3 – Part 3: The Gospel of God
   TR4 – Resources and Appendices

Theological Handbooks (TH)

   TH1 – Part 1: The Way of God
   TH2 – Part 2
   TH3 – Part 3

www.DaystarInstituteNM.us   WalkingintheWayUSA@gmail.com

www.ingramcontent.com/pod-product-compliance
Lightning Source LLC
Chambersburg PA
CBHW071935020426
42331CB00010B/2884